Songbirds

Edited by
Lynn Hughes

Workman Publishing
New York

Library of Congress Cataloging in Publication Data

Main entry under title:

Songbirds.

1. Birds — Literary collections. 2. Birds in art.
I. Hughes, Lynn.
PS509.B5S6   810'.8'036   81-40509
ISBN 0-89480-189-9   AACR2

Picture research by Ian Wyles

Workman Publishing
1 West 39 Street
New York, New York 10018

Manufactured in the United States of America
First printing August 1981
10 9 8 7 6 5 4 3 2 1

Songbirds

To hear the lark begin his flight,
And singing startle the dull night;
From his watch tower in the skies,
Till the dappled dawn doth rise.

MILTON
L'ALLEGRO

THE SKYLARK.

A birdie with a yellow bill
Hopped upon the window sill,
Cocked his shining eye and said:
'Ain't you 'shamed, you sleepy-head?'

ROBERT LOUIS STEVENSON
TIME TO RISE

TOWN SPARROW.
MALE & FEMALE

The nest of the mavis
Is in the bonnie copse,
My little one will sleep
    and he shall have the bird.
The nest of the blackbird
Is in the withered bough,
My little one will sleep
    and he shall have the bird.
The nest of the cuckoo
Is in the hedge-sparrows nest,
My little one will sleep
    and he will have the bird.
The nest of the kite
Is high on the mountain-slope,
My little one will sleep
    and he shall have the bird.

ANON
GAELIC LULLABY

The thrush which sang to me an hour
Sang with artistry and power.
From the highest branches of the tree
He undid the lock of minstrelsy.
The prophet of passion and love and desire
Is our minstrel chief in his woodland choir.
The voices by the whispering stream
He takes into his lusty theme;
In him there's a song of ecstasy;
In him an organ strain maybe,
And all the songs of loved or lover
In him contend for ever.
He sings the song of every bird,
And when at evening he has heard
The rapturous lovers in the glade,
He sings at dusk his serenade.
But most he's the preacher; his muse is there,
And he reads his lesson loud and clear.
He is the chief of the minstrels of May,
The song of Ovid his roundelay.
Where the hazels tangle a song he sings,
The song of an angel, on angel's wings.
'Tis rarely falls from Paradise,
In ecstasy remembering,
A bird who knows its melodies
And can that angel music sing.

DAFYDD AP GWILYM
THE THRUSH IN SONG

It certainly was a remarkable provision of Nature to assign to the same species of animal both song and flight: so that those which had to cheer other living things with the voice should be usually aloft: whence the sound could spread around through a greater space, and reach a greater number of hearers; and so that the air, which is the element destined for sound, should be populous with vocal and musical creatures.

GIACOMO LEOPARDI
ELOGIO DEGLI UCCELLI

Ay, little larky! what's the reason,
Singing thus in winter season?
Nothing, surely, can be pleasing
   To make thee sing;
For I see naught but cold and freezing,
   And feel its sting.
Perhaps, all done with silent mourning,
Thou think'st that summer is returning,
And this the last, cold, frosty morning,
   To chill thy breast;
If so, I pity thy discerning:
   And so I've guess'd.
Poor little songster! vainly cheated,
Stay, leave thy singing uncompleted,
Drop where thou wast beforehand seated,
   In thy warm nest;
Nor let vain wishes be repeated,
   But sit at rest.

JOHN CLARE
ADDRESS TO A LARK
SINGING IN WINTER

Somewhere afield here something lies
In Earth's oblivious eyeless trust
That moved a poet to prophecies -
A pinch of unseen, unguarded dust:
The dust of the lark that Shelley heard,
And made immortal through times to be; -
Though it only lived like another bird,
And knew not its immortality:
Lived its meek life; then, one day, fell -
A little ball of feather and bone;
And how it perished, when piped farewell,
And where it wastes, are alike unknown.
Maybe it rests in the loam I view,
Maybe it throbs in a myrtle's green,
Maybe it sleeps in the coming hue
Of a grape on the slopes of yon inland scene.
Go find it, faeries, go and find
That tiny pinch of priceless dust,
And bring a casket silver-lined,
And framed of gold that gems encrust;
And we will lay it safe therein,
And consecrate it to endless time;
For it inspired a bard to win
Ecstatic heights in thought and rhyme.

THOMAS HARDY
SHELLEY'S SKYLARK

The breezy call of incense-breathing Morn,
  The swallow twitt'ring from the straw-built
                                    shed,
The cock's shrill clarion, or the echoing horn,
  No more shall rouse them from their lowly
                                    bed.

THOMAS GRAY
ELEGY WRITTEN IN
A COUNTRY CHURCHYARD

'Summer is coming, summer is coming,
     I know it, I know it, I know it.
Light again, leaf again, life again, love
          again,'
     Yes, my wild little Poet.
Sing the new year in under the blue,
     Last year you sang it as gladly.
'New, new, new, new'! Is it then so new
     That you should carol so madly?
'Love again, song again, nest again, young
          again.'
     Never a prophet so crazy!
And hardly a daisy as yet, little friend,
     See, there is hardly a daisy.
'Here again, here, here, here, happy
          year'!
     O warble unchidden, unbidden!
Summer is coming, is coming, my dear,
     And all the winters are hidden.

                              TENNYSON
                              THE THROSTLE

Of all our wild birds none is known to be of a more affectionate disposition than our little blackcap. Its love for its mate is very tender; and its solicitude for her and its young is most marked. When the young ones quit the nest, they will all follow the parent birds, hopping from branch to branch, in company; and at night the whole family perch on one branch, a parent bird at each end, guarding the young ones which are placed in the middle. They seem to dislike cold, for they all press closely against each other; and the blackcap when kept in a cage spreads some of its feathers over its feet to keep them warm.

ANNE PRATT
OUR NATIVE SONGSTERS

And sedge-warblers, clinging so light
To willow twigs, sang longer than the lark,
Quick, shrill, or grating, a song to match the heat
Of the strong sun, nor less the water's cool,
Gushing through narrows, swirling in the pool.
Their song that lacks all words, all melody,
All sweetness almost, was dearer then to me
Than sweetest voice that sings in tune sweet
    words.
This was the best of May – the small brown birds
Wisely reiterating endlessly
What no man learnt yet, in or out of school.

EDWARD THOMAS
SEDGE-WARBLERS

AEDON GALACTODES.

Teevo cheevo cheevio chee:
O where, what can that be?
Weedio-weedio: there again!
So tiny a trickle of sóng-strain;
And all round not to be found
For brier, bough, furrow, or gréen ground
Before or behind or far or at hand
Either left either right
Anywhere in the súnlight.
Well, after all! Ah but hark –
'I am the little wóodlark.
The skylark is my cousin and he
Is known to men more than me.
Round a ring, around a ring
And while I sail (must listen) I sing.
   And down . . . the furrow dry
   Sunspurge and oxeye
   And lace-leaved lovely
   Foam-tuft fumitory.
Through the velvety wind V-winged
[Where shake shadow is sun's-eye-ringed]
To the nest's nook I balance and buoy
With a sweet joy of a sweet joy,
Sweet, of a sweet, of a sweet joy
Of a sweet-a sweet-sweet-joy.'

GERARD MANLEY HOPKINS
THE WOODLARK

As it fell upon a day,
In the merry month of May,
Sitting in a pleasant shade,
Which a grove of myrtles made.
Beasts did leap and birds did sing,
Trees did grow and plants did spring,
Everything did banish moan,
Save the nightingale alone.
She, poor bird, as all forlorn,
Lean'd her breast up-till a thorn,
And there sung the dolefull'st ditty
That to hear it was great pity.
Fie, fie, fie, now would she cry;
Tereu, Tereu, by and by.

RICHARD BARNFIELD
IN DIVERS HUMORS

But the Nightingale, another of my airy creatures, breathes such sweet loud musick out of her little instrumental throat, that it might make mankind to think miracles are not ceased. He that at midnight, when the very labourer sleeps securely, should hear, as I have very often, the clear airs, the sweet descants, the natural rising and falling, the doubling and redoubling of her voice, might well be lifted above earth, and say, 'Lord, what musick hast thou provided for the Saints in Heaven, when thou affordest bad men such musick on Earth!'

ISAAC WALTON
THE COMPLEAT ANGLER

Dear, dear, dear,
In the rocky glen,
Far away, far away, far away
The haunts of men;
There shall we dwell in love.
With the lark and the dove,
Cuckoo and corn-rail,
Feast on the bearded snail,
Worm and gilded fly,
Drink of the crystal rill
Winding adown the hill
Never to dry.
With glee, with glee, with glee
   Cheer up, cheer up, cheer up here;
Nothing to harm us, then sing merrily,
   Sing to the loved one whose nest is near.

ANON
THE THRUSH'S SONG
(Gaelic 9th Century)

O blackbird, what a boy you are!
How you do go it.

T. E. BROWN
THE BLACKBIRD

O to be in England
Now that April's there,
And whoever wakes in England
Sees, some morning, unaware,
That the lowest boughs and the brushwood sheaf
Round the elm-tree bole are in tiny leaf,
While the chaffinch sings on the orchard bough
In England - now!

And after April, when May follows,
And the whitethroat builds, and all the swallows!
Hark, where my blossom'd pear-tree in the hedge
Leans to the field and scatters on the clover
Blossoms and dewdrops - at the bent spray's
     edge-
That's the wise thrush; he sings each song twice
     over,
Lest you should think he never could recapture
The first fine careless rapture!
And though the fields look rough with hoary
     dew,
All will be gay when noontide wakes anew
The buttercups, the little children's dower
- Far brighter than this gaudy melon-flower!

ROBERT BROWNING
HOME-THOUGHTS, FROM ABROAD

J. Gould and H.C. Richter del. et lith.   SYLVIA CINEREA.   W. Etts lim.

The marsh warbler is a merry bird, singing all day long and easily urged into song, if, when it chance to be silent, a stone is thrown at it. Away it glides then into some deeper recess among the water plants, and commencing its rapid strain seems to bid cheerful defiance to fear and danger: then it gives the whit, whit, whit of the swallow, or the twink, twink, twink of the chaffinch, to perfection; or suddenly it utters the chur-r-r, chur-r-r, which is its own sound, if any danger is apprehended to its nest from an approaching footstep. Its singing is very singular as it sounds forth from the reedy waters late at night when hundreds of voices seem sometimes joining in concert, and the traveller at that lone hour listens with wonder and pleasure to the strange tones.

ANNE PRATT
OUR NATIVE SONGSTERS

In Scotland the yellowhammer sings, 'Whetil te, whetil te, whee! Harry my nest, and the de'il tak ye,' and the bird is called 'De'il, de'il, de'il take ye!' The malediction which the yellow yorling utters has not prevented its persecution. Boys used to play 'periwinkie' with its eggs, whacking blindfold at them with a stick. In Denmark a sufferer from jaundice is advised to eat three yellowhammers, including feathers and bones. This is probably a jocular suggestion inspired by mediaeval beliefs that birds with yellow markings (such as the yellow-eyed stone curlew) were effective medicinally against this malady. The sinister significance of the colour yellow still survives in the use of a yellow flag as a signal of quarantine.

EDWARD A. ARMSTRONG
THE FOLKLORE OF BIRDS

When little more than two months old, they begin to whistle, and then their training as pipers must commence. This tuition, among professional bullfinch-trainers, is systematic. They have schools of birds, which are kept unfed for a longer time than they have been accustomed to, and they are placed in a darkened room. The bird is wakeful and attentive from the want of his food, and the tune he is to learn is played several times on an instrument made for the purpose, and known as a bird-organ, its notes resembling those of the bullfinch. For an hour or two the young pupils mope silently, but they gradually begin to imitate the notes of the music played to them. When one commences – and he is looked upon as the most likely to make a good piper – the others soon follow his example. The light is then admitted and a portion of food, but not a full meal, is given to the birds. Thus, by degrees, by the playing on the bird-organ, by the admission of light, which is always agreeable to the finch, and by the reward of more and more, and sometimes more relishable food, the pupil 'practises' the notes he hears continuously.

HENRY MAYHEW
LONDON LABOUR AND
THE LONDON POOR

Sadly the ousel sings. I know
No less than he a world of woe.
The robbers of his nest have ta'en
His eggs and all his younglings slain.
The grief his sobbing notes would say
I knew it but the other day:
Sad ousel, well I know that tone
Of sorrow for thy nestlings gone.

ANON
FROM LEBAR BREC
(Irish 11th Century)

They are accustomed in Pembrokeshire to carry a wren in a bier on Twelfth Night; from a young man to his sweetheart, that is two or three bear it in a bier (covered) with ribbons, and sing carols. They also go to other houses where there are no sweethearts and there will be beer etc. And the bier from the country they call Cutty Wran.

EDWARD LHUYD
PAROCHIALIA

THE WREN.

The bank swallows veer and dip,
Diving down at my windows,
Then flying almost straight upward,
Like bats in daytime,
And their shadows, bigger,
Race over the thick grass;
And the finches pitch through the air, twittering;
And the small mad siskins flit by,
Flying upward in little skips and erratic leaps;
Or they sit sideways on limber dandelion stems,
Bending them down to the ground;
Or perch and peck at larger flower-crowns,
Springing, one to another,
The last-abandoned stalk always quivering
Back into straightness;
Or they fling themselves against tree trunks,
Scuttling down and around like young squirrels,
Birds furious as bees.
Now they move all together! –
These airy hippety-hop skippers,
Light as seed blowing off thistles!
And I seem to lean forward,
As my eyes follow after
Their sunlip leaping.

THEODORE ROETHKE
THE SISKINS

I leant upon a coppice gate
    When Frost was spectre-gray,
And Winter's dregs made desolate
    The weakening eye of day.
The tangled bine-stems scored the sky
    Like strings of broken lyres,
And all mankind that haunted nigh
    Had sought their household fires.

At once a voice arose among
    The bleak twigs overhead
In a full-hearted evensong
    Of joy illimited;
An aged thrush, frail, gaunt, and small,
    In blast-beruffled plume,
Had chosen thus to fling his soul
    Upon the growing gloom.

So little cause for carolings
    Of such ecstatic sound
Was written on terrestrial things
    Afar or nigh around,
That I could think there trembled through
    His happy good-night air
Some blessed Hope, whereof he knew
    And I was unaware.

THOMAS HARDY
THE DARKLING THRUSH

Goodbye, goodbye to summer!
　　For summer's nearly done;
The garden smiling faintly,
　　Cool breezes in the sun;
Our thrushes now are silent,
　　Our swallows flown away –
But Robin's here, in coat of brown,
　　With ruddy breast-knot gay.
Robin, Robin Redbreast,
　　O Robin dear!
Robin singing sweetly
　　In the falling of the year.
The fireside for the cricket,
　　The wheatstack for the mouse,
When trembling night-winds whistle
　　And moan all round the house;
The frosty ways like iron,
　　The branches plumed with snow –
Alas! in winter, dead and dark,
　　Where can poor Robin go?
Robin, Robin Redbreast,
　　O Robin dear!
And a crumb of bread for Robin,
　　His little heart to cheer.

WILLIAM ALLINGHAM
ROBIN REDBREAST

Keulemans lith.   Hart

PERSIAN ROBIN
ERITHACUS HYRCANUS

Illustration acknowledgments

The author and publisher gratefully acknowledge the following for permission to use copyright material:

Dr Ann Ross, Alexander Carmichael and the Editors of *Carmina Gadelica* for 'Gaelic Lullaby'; The Honorable Society of Cymmrodorion and the estate of the late David Bell for 'The Thrush in Song' translated from the Welsh of Dafydd ap Gwilym; Macmillan and Co. Ltd for Thomas Hardy's 'The Darkling Thrush' and 'Shelley's Skylark'; Mrs Myfannwy Thomas and Faber and Faber Ltd for 'Sedge Warblers' by Edward Thomas; William Collins Ltd for 'The Folklore of Birds' by Edward Armstrong; Doubleday and Co. Inc for 'The Siskins' by Theodore Roethke.